First printing, 2021.

Brian D. Wilson
2056 Ammen Road
Fincastle, VA 24090

https://innerpixel.org/

INNER
PIXEL

compiled by

01000010 01110010 01101001 01100001 01101110
00100000 01000100 00100000 01010111 01101001
01101100 01110011 01101111 01101110

Hello, I'm Peter Pixel,
and I live inside a screen,
with tons of other pixels.
It's a pretty crowded scene.

00001

In case you didn't know it,
every pixel is a dot,
Each one of us is tiny,
so we're kind of hard to spot.

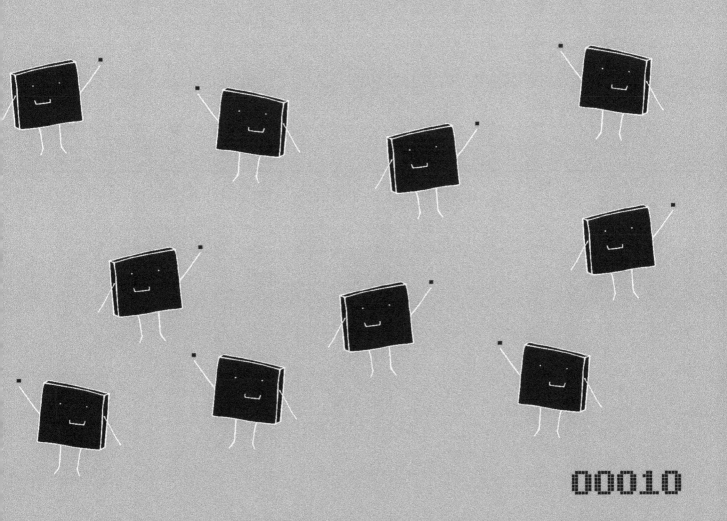

00010

On computers, phones, and tablets
you will always find us there,
creating words and images
from rectangles and squares.

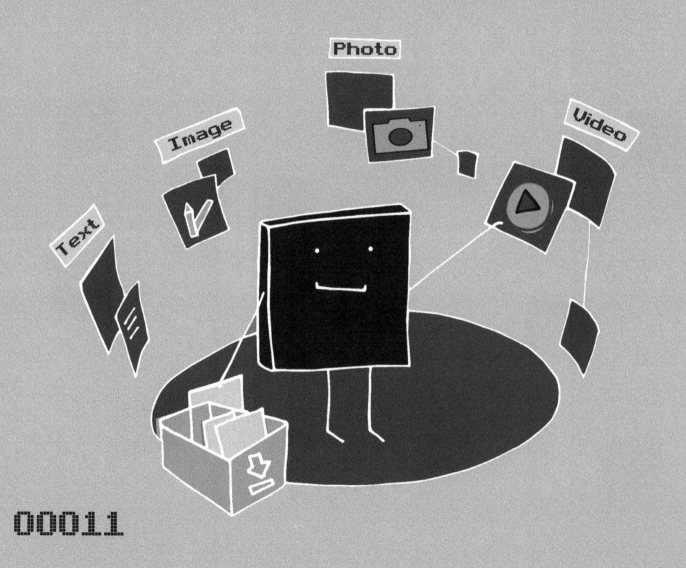

00011

I tried to make an image
with some pixels just like me,
But when we got together,
there was nothing there to see.

00100

To make a perfect picture,
you can never work alone.
Without the other colors,
you'll be no good on your own.

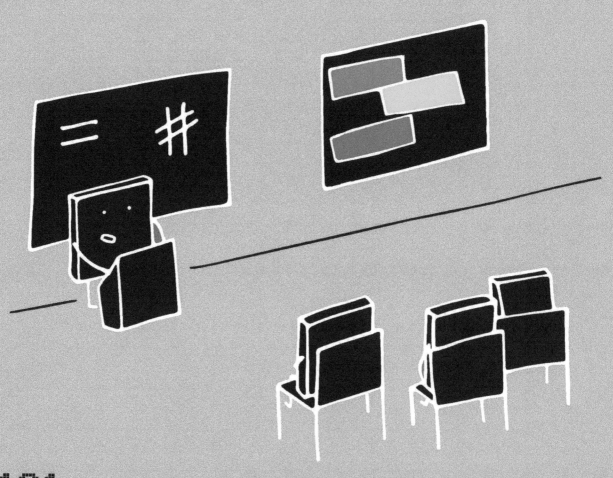

00101

A blackened bunch of pixels,
whether long, or short, or tall,
were invisible to people.
We could not be seen at all.

00110

We just sat there feeling silly,
with the screen as black as night.
Till another pixel came along,
whose name was Wally White.

00111

So I asked if he would help me
jot some numbers on the screen.
And sure enough, hey, presto!
Every digit could be seen.

01000

So next we wrote some letters
just to see if they'd appear.
And there upon the monitor,
the words were crystal clear.

01001

In black and white, the images
looked good in every way.
A perfect pixel partnership
on digital display.

01010

That night I went to sleep
and had a multi-colored dream.
Perhaps some other pixel friends
would like to join the team?

01100

So off we went to Gary Green's
when breakfast time was done.
And Gary was delighted
to be joining in the fun.

01100

He called his cousin up as well.
"She'll help us out," he said.
So off we went to Pixel Street
to pick up Cherry Red.

01101

With all the pixels side-by-side,
we had a team of four.
"I'll tell you what," I said to them.
"I think we need one more?"

01110

"You could be right," said Cherry Red,
"I know exactly who.
I'm going to text him right away.
His name is Barry Blue."

01111

With our little Pixel army,
it was time for us to start,
"Let's make a picture now," I said.
"We'll use this color chart."

There are more than 16 million
different colors we could make.
But Gary said, "No way, Jose.
We'll never stay awake."

10001

"Yes, that would take forever,"
Cherry Red said with a sigh. "
I know, let's make a rainbow
stretching right across the sky."

10010

"Now did you know? said Wally.
"And I think that this is true.
On the inside, every pixel's
colored red and green and blue."

10011

We can switch to different colors
with the changing of the light.
That's except for me and Peter,
who are always black or white."

10100

"That's interesting," I told him.
"I could listen on for hours.
But it's time we made a picture
using all our pixel powers."

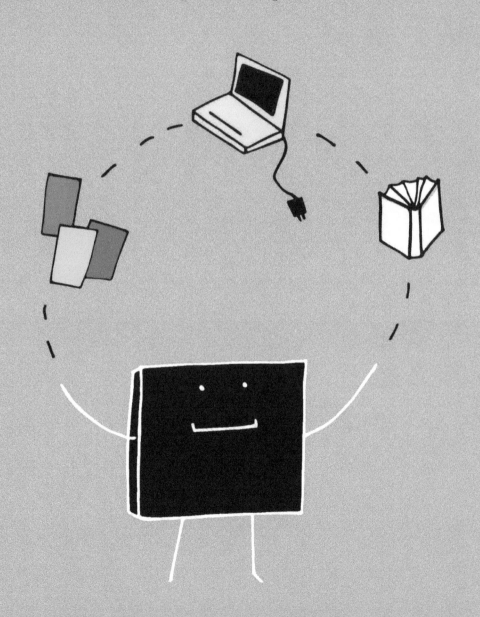

10101

So we started getting busy
in the back of the machine,
making all the rainbow colors
which appeared upon the screen.

10110

There was red, and there was orange.
There was yellow, green, and blue
There was indigo and violet,
that's a purple-colored hue.

10111

And the rainbow we created
was a splendid sight to see.
"It's gorgeous," Barry Blue announced.
And all of us agreed.

11000

"We worked together very well,"
   I told my pixel friends.
"It's better when you share the load,
   on that you can depend."

11001

CPSIA information can be obtained
at www.ICGtesting.com
Printed in the USA
LVHW071151030322
712537LV00002B/17